A ROOKIE READER™

MICE!

By Julie E. Frankel

Illustrations by Mike Venezia

Prepared under the direction of Robert Hillerich, Ph.D.

CHILDRENS PRESS ®

CHICAGO

Library of Congress Cataloging in Publication Data

Frankel, Julie E.
  Mice.

  (A Rookie Reader)
  Summary: Easy text and illustrations describe the
activities of a variety of mice. Includes a list of words
used in the text.
  [1. Mice—Fiction] I. Venezia, Mike, ill. II. Title.
III. Series.
PZ7.F8545Mi 1986   [E]   86-1008
ISBN 0-516-02070-6

Mice!!

3

Where?

4

Here?

No, there!

In?

No, out!

Up?

No, down!

Over?

No, under!

Slow?

No, fast!

17

A few?

19

No, many!

Black?

No, gray!

Big?

No, small! No, wait. . .

. . . none at all!

No mice?

28

No mice.

That's nice!

31

WORD LIST

a	here	over
all	in	slow
at	many	small
big	mice	that's
black	nice	there
down	no	under
fast	none	wait
few	out	where
gray		

About the Author

Julie E. Frankel was born and raised in St. Louis, Missouri. she has a Bachelor of Science Degree in Education with an endorsement in Early Childhood, a Master of Arts in Teaching Degree in Communications, and is now teaching first grade. Besides writing for children, Julie enjoys photography, travel, theater, music, and people. Julie's first book is dedicated to her family and friends.

About the Artist

Mice! is the eighth book illustrated by **Mike Venezia** for Childrens Press. The others are *Sometimes I Worry, What If The Teacher Calls On Me?, Ask A Silly Question, Rugs Have Naps, The I Don't Want To Go To School Book, How to Be an Older Brother or Sister,* and *Eat Your Peas, Louise!*. Mike is a graduate of the School of The Art Institute of Chicago. When not working on children's books, Mike is a busy Chicago art director and father of Michael Anthony and Elizabeth Ann.